Dedication

To the many parishioners of Our Lady of the Angels
Parish, Kenai, Alaska, whose loving and thoughtful
responses to our questionnaire were the foundation
and impetus to do this work.

To the Sullivans,

With gratitude,

Sister Joyce Ross

Sr. Joan Barina

Map of Alaska

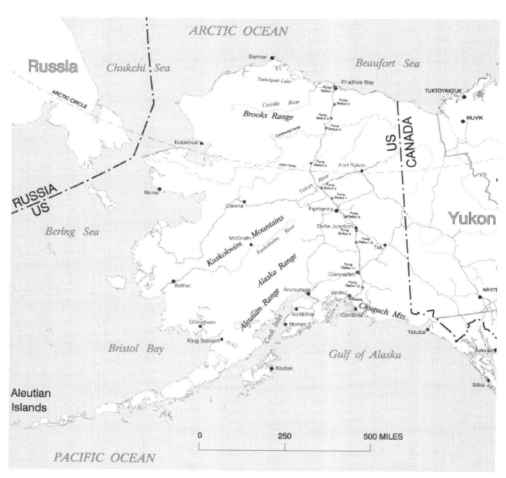

Table of Contents

Southeast Alaska - Valdez
Yukon - Kuskowim Delta
Talkeetna
Other Places
Albany

Forward

My ministry in the Church began in 1957, shortly before the Second Vatican Council.

Given the long history of the predominance of priests at the liturgy and in pastoral work generally, it never occurred to me that this model of ministry would ever change. Indeed, one would hardly dare give any thought to such a possibility. It was too well established a tradition.

As some of the documents of the Second Vatican Council began to trickle out, however, it suddenly became clear to us that there was a different perception of ministry in general and the role of the laity in particular. In such documents as Apostolicum Actuositatem (Decree on the Apostolate of Lay People), Gaudium et Spes (The Pastoral Constitution on the Church in the Modern World) and Lumen Gentium (Dogmatic Constitution on the Church) gave clear evidence that a new sense of Church was in the works. Phrases such as "People of God" and "Roles of the Laity" became common usage. One gradually began to have the sense that the role of the lay people in the liturgy was not simply one of "helping father" but rather that lay people should now be considered full and rightful cooperators in the work of the Church by the very reason of their baptismal character. All this was new to us in the late 60's and we were gratified that the gifts of the laity were finally being recognized.

The question that remained however, was this: in what sort of framework should the work of the laity be implemented? Gradually, of course, we reflect on the progress of lay involvement, such ministries as lector, Eucharistic minister, ministers to the sick and dying, prison ministry, et cetera seemed appropriate and were soon implemented.

What was left unsaid, of course, was the question of direct involvement in leadership roles, whether liturgical or administrative. At that point no need was seen for parish administrators, pastoral leaders, pastoral associates; there were still abundant priests to take responsibility for such roles.

In the past 40 years since the conclusion of the Council, social and ecclesiastical structures have changed radically. The numbers of priests has radically declined, so radically, indeed that it became obvious that a different sort of ministry would need to be called into service.

Unfortunately, however, it took an unforeseen turn of events to bring the role of the laity into focus. One might have expected that over time the hopes and ideals of the Council would have been naturally and logically implemented by way of theological and liturgical development.

Speaking for myself in terms of my pastoral assignments, I was fortunate to be assigned to the Archdiocese of Anchorage for a period of years. It was here that I finally saw the hopes of the Council flourish in ways I had never imagined.

Obviously, Alaska being a remote territory, has never developed an on going process of seeking vocation prospects. As a result, many of the parishes in outlying areas of the state had never had the availability of a permanent pastor. From the earliest times, traveling priests made up the bulk of pastoral service. Even so, with the decline of priests, the need was seen for a local person (mainly lay women and religious) to take over the responsibility of pasturing these remote parishes.

Many people living in large cities around the country were quick to say "This will never work". Women do not have pastoral skills to "Run a parish". Moreover, it was pointed out that so-called "communion services", which were becoming more and more frequent, did not satisfy the need for the celebration of the Eucharist as we know it theologically and traditionally, True enough.

It has been my experience, however, being privileged to work closely with pastoral administrators for many years, that these women possessed a sense of Church and a sense of pastoral responsibility that priest-pastors often lacked.

I found it quite normal to work hand in hand with these religious. The dedicated work that they did to call community together for worship, see to administrative responsibilities, visit the sick and the homebound, form active pastoral councils, in short, to form true Christian community, all these were obviously as effective in forming Church as any I have observed in parishes administered by a priest pastor.

Additionally, it became evident to me that religious sisters and laywomen administering parishes had a certain pastoral instinct that many priests had never learned or had long forgotten.

My point in all this is that in many of these small parishes without a priest, there was a certain common sense responsibility on the part of parishioners. "It's nice to have a priest on Sunday", they would often say, but our lay minister or religious sister is dedicated to us at all times. They have taught us how to form community and to take the normal responsibilities that in many cases a priest would take care of. In short, it was Vatican II in action.

Finally, it is my perception that the pastoral administration (for lack of a better title) had an intuitive sense of church and were gratified to be able to carry out their responsibilities as baptized Christians.

For those who said "This form of ministry will never work," I say, "I saw it working. I am convinced that it is the form of ministry for the years ahead. Even should there be a sudden influx of vocations to the priesthood, the Church will never find it's true goal, as outlined in the documents of the Council unless priests, nuns, and lay people work together to bring about the Kingdom that Jesus said would come.

LeRoy E. Clememtich, C.S.C.
Notre Dame, Indiana
March 31, 2010

Why Write This Book?

"Now to him who by the power at work within us is able to accomplish abundantly far more than all we can ask or imagine, to him be glory in the church and in Christ Jesus to all generations, forever and ever. Amen"
Eph.3:20-21

In telling the story of our experience of the church in Kenai and Alaska, we hope the above question will be answered. We believe that the teaching of Vatican II on the laity as the People of God and as "Church" is clear and is expressed by the people in the pages that follow.

Because of the remoteness of many places in Alaska and the need of the people to "make do" in certain circumstances, they used their ingenuity to create communities of faith, maintaining and helping them grow. This tendency continued even when priests were available some weekends. Since there was no resident priest, it was up to the parishioners to do the needful, from maintaining the plant to planning building expansion, from liturgical to social and outreach programs.

When a parish is without a resident priest, the choice of director or leader is very important. The consultation of parishioners in this decision is crucial. In our case at a town hall type meeting with Archbishop Hurley, the parishioners were very helpful. Since we had been working there ten years, the majority of the parishioners knew us; voiced their approval and subsequently were very cooperative. We felt it gave the people a much greater sense of ownership in the parish.

Another important aspect of our journey was obtaining input from the major players, the parishioners of Our Lady of the Angels. We designed a questionnaire to reveal their understanding of the major changes occurring in our church. (Please consult the sample copy of the questions in the back of this chapter.) One of the first questions asked was how they felt about being in or joining a parish without a resident priest. Many had experienced the Church in Alaska without the privilege of a resident priest, especially in isolated areas, so were not alarmed at the prospect of joining such a parish.

A coast guard wife wrote, "Even before I arrived, I knew there was no resident priest and so I was curious how different 'going to church' would be. My reaction to my first liturgy with no priest was surprise, I was surprised to discover 'real communion'. My experience deepened as I went from attending Mass to active listening more as a participator than an attendee in the liturgy, 'the prayer of the people'".

This was no ordinary parish. The more I became involved the deeper my understanding was of what it meant to be "Church" honoring and sharing each others' gifts was the norm" [1]

This outstanding parishioner developed her gifts to become one of the lay persons conducting communion services for the parish on weekends when a priest was not available and was a true spiritual director and guide.

Those who did not experience a parish without a resident priest had different reactions. Some of their responses are listed below:

"When we first came to Kenai we were aware that there was not a resident priest. We did come to realize that though you need a priest to say a Mass, you do not necessarily need a priest to run a parish."2

"When we started to attend church my wife and I found out that there was not a resident priest, I accepted it without question, because here in Alaska, we are used to 'making do' with what we have. It is part of our 'can do' attitude."3

"Time proved that a parish doesn't have to have a priest, but a dedicated leader and willing members to be a great parish community."4

This is from a young parishioner, now a college student; "When my family and I first attended Our Lady of the Angels I was a naïve fifth grader who thought nothing odd about a church lacking a resident priest. It never crossed my mind that a church normally has resident priests. On the contrary, I considered the visiting priests and our very own Sister's homilies a normal part of the church experience. Hearing different sermon styles and unique homily approaches was eye opening and wonderfully diverse. Indeed my initial interpretation toward visiting priests never changed; instead I grew to appreciate them more. I honestly felt blessed for the opportunity to hear such a wide variety of worldly minded and intellectual preachers."5

Other qualities in the Kenai parish attracted newcomers. Some respondents expressed that the reason they joined our parish was because of the reception they received there.

"I guess that we can honestly say that we did not think much about the fact that there was no resident priest because we judged how we thought we would fit into the family by the way we were welcomed and accepted."6

"Everyone in Kenai was so warm and welcoming... we really felt a connection to the other parishioners and started getting more involved in things like Bible study groups, the Faith Formation program, and helping with Clothes Quarters (thrift store) and counting contributions. We feel like we not only belonged to this parish but are part of the parish. We are a Community. We are the church."2

This is my thought in reflecting on these responses; because of our years of experience in the parish, the depth and honesty shown in the responses did not surprise us but inspired us. These parishioners had taken the teaching of Vatican II to heart and acted on it.

Questionnaire sent to parishioners

Dear Parishioners,

After living and working on the Kenai, we have learned much about Church as defined by Vatican II, "The Church is the People of God", in other words, "We are the Church".

We also realize that not everyone understands the full impact of what that means. You have taught us what being church for each other can be and we would like to share these insights of church with others by writing about it. We would appreciate your help in doing this by answering the following questions.
You were living in the parish before the sisters took over. What were your feelings at the time of thee announcement? Did these feelings change as time went on? In what way?

Or

At the time you moved into Kenai and found the parish did not have a resident priest, what was your reaction? Did it change as time passed? What were your thoughts about being church as you got involved in the parish?

Has the past twenty years changed your definition and attitude about being church? Will you continue to be that church now that you have priests? Why or why not?

Lastly, has this experience changed your attitude toward Eucharist? If so, in what way? May we quote you if necessary?

Thank you for your help, especially in sharing your understandings and insights about these important faith issues. We continue to keep you in our prayers.

God bless,

Sister Joyce and Sister Joan

Notes:
1.   Valerie Kwietniak
2.   Karla Smith
3.   Clifford Smith
4.   Jeanette Neel
5.   Kristi Louthan
6.   Sal and Kathy Mattero

Study questions

- What do you think your reaction would be if your parish would have no resident priest?
- Have you pondered what it means to be the "people of God?" What conclusions have you come to?

The Journey Begins

After this the Lord appointed seventy others and sent them ahead of him in pairs Luke-10:1

In October of 1978, Archbishop Francis T. Hurley called on Sister Joyce Ross to ask her to consider becoming Religious Education Director for the Parishes on the Kenai Peninsula. She had enjoyed her seven years at St. Patrick's but the prospect of something new was interesting. The Mercy Leaders, Sisters Martha Joyce and Karen Marcil came for their visitation; a meeting was held and plans for the move were made. No Sister of Mercy was available to work with Sister Joyce. Sister Joan Barina, a Medical Mission Sister was living at the time with the Mercies in Anchorage. Sister Joan was working at the Native Hospital as a medical technologist, but was ready for a career change. Sister Joyce knew this and asked the Bishop for permission to approach Sister Joan about doing parish work. He answered, "Work it out with your communities". After checking with their superiors, they committed themselves to working on the Peninsula. Plans were made, meetings with the Redemptorist priests who were the pastors were held and the Sisters left for Kenai on August 1, 1979.

It was a three hour drive south to the Kenai; it was a beautiful day and the scenery was spectacular. There were no houses for rent at the time, so a basement apartment was secured by the parishes. The apartment was halfway between Kenai and Soldotna (towns thirteen miles apart).

An agreement was made that if the place didn't work out, the sisters could look for more suitable quarters after a year.

Saturday was the day of arrival, so the sisters attended the six o'clock Mass in Kenai. Father Robert Wells, the pastor welcomed them. He and three families from the parish helped them to unload their belongings. A van from Anchorage was donated by Bill and Linda Garland from St. Patrick's in Anchorage. With all the help it took little time to unload the truck and settle the house. The women made up the beds and did all the nice and practical things women think of and do. Everything was settled in no time.

As the transition began the sisters realized the importance of meeting the parishioners and learning about each parish. They began by attending Mass in Kenai where they received a warm welcome. The same was true when they went to Homer.

Soldotna and Seward parishes were a little different. The welcome was polite; it was evident that the pastors accepted sisters because the Bishop sent them. It's understandable that people would question why, after all the parishioners had been running their own programs successfully since the early 1960's. How they reacted was understandable. It was the sister's job to prove they were resource people. They were there to help, not replace. It seemed to work and after the first year all were working together.

Because of stepping lightly the first year the sisters did a lot of exploring on the Peninsula and a lot of fishing. This caused Sister Joan some apprehension, but Sister Joyce having served in small towns before said, "Don't worry about it, someday we won't have time to fish or play." Truer words were never spoken because in their later years the sisters were too busy to fish.

They visited each parish once a month. Travel was the name of the game. It is eighty miles to Homer and about forty to Ninilchik. Mostly, the programs went well; families learning together was the goal. The sisters met with parents and they in turn taught their children. Seward was a struggle; after driving about two hours or so on slippery hilly roads to get around the peninsula, the sisters found that some people weren't willing to drive six miles to attend the programs. It was discouraging.

The first year of the adventure in Kenai taught the sisters a lot about driving on ice and in the dark. In winter in South Central Alaska it's dark about twenty hours a day.

The area where they lived was out of town and wooded, so moose often wandered by. Skiing out their front door and spotting one of these huge animals was not unusual. It was easy to think of them as "our moose", but hitting one on the road would have been very upsetting; thank God for sparing them that experience.

Snow and below freezing temperatures were common. Many days the car would not start or they got stuck. Like all Alaskans the sisters became adept at pulling through berms left by the plows and recovering from spinning wheels. They could usually get going without help when they got stuck in snow. No small accomplishment! To get to Anchorage or Seward you drive through the Chugach Mountains therefore avalanches were always a possibility. Only once going to Anchorage did the sisters get caught between two avalanches. It was an interesting experience waiting for the road to be open. It was the only time they were between two; other times they either turned around or waited while the road was being plowed.

Spring was delightful. During May the sisters took vacation by going to visit family and community; New York for Sr. Joyce and Wisconsin for Sr. Joan. Returning in early June when the days are long (20 hours) and everything is green has special meaning to Alaskans after the darkness and cold. People were glad to see them and the most common greeting was "You came back." It was a good beginning to a long and fruitful ministry on the Kenai Peninsula in the State of Alaska.

In 1980-81 the mission in Kenai and Homer went well. Overnight accommodations were always a surprise. In the beginning in Homer the sisters stayed in the Pick and Pay building. This was the second hand clothing store run by the Ladies Guild. There was a spare room off the shop area that was adequate, but had no water. Nightly ablutions were taken in the church basement. For a time meals were in the rectory, but it was not really convenient for the pastor or the sisters. Most of the time they ate out, on occasion parishioners would ask them to dinner. Later John and Viola Hansen from Anchor Point offered them hospitality and the sister stayed with them for years. They became good friends of the sisters who always looked forward to good meals and a good Scrabble game at their home.

In Seward the rectory was central both for sleeping and meals. The priest was happy to have the sisters cook, but was uncomfortable with the sisters in the next bedroom. Eventually, the situation worked itself out; their services were no longer needed in Seward.

After a year in the basement apartment it was time to move. There were a few disadvantages. Since the apartment was between Kenai and Soldotna the sisters felt like they really didn't belong in either place. To live in one town or the other was preferable. Both the sisters and the priests came to that conclusion. Also, living in a basement in Alaska where the snow covers the windows in an already dark winter is somewhat depressing. However, finding a new home was still a challenge.

There was only one house for rent listed in the paper. It was in Kenai, and fortunately owned by parishioners. It was about one mile from church in the Woodland subdivision. The couple was willing to rent to them for five hundred dollars a month, take care of maintenance, lawn mowing and snow removal.

In August the parishioners helped the sisters to move. The owners expected to be gone for seven years. However, the husband was transferred overseas and the couple decided to sell. Luckily the parish council, at the urging of Sally Bailey, decided it was best to buy the house. The sisters were delighted.

After having observed the religion programs for a year, the sisters were convinced that some changes needed to be made. The coordinator in Soldotna resigned; she had the responsibility for many years and felt it was time. Kay Meteer accepted the position graciously. The Kenai coordinator, Marge O'Reilly had the position because it was part of her parish council responsibility. Her term was up. She felt that the coordinator should not be picked from the council, but should be someone who wanted the position and could devote more time to it. The coordinator would be ex-officio on the council. The council agreed and Judy Dragseth became director in the Kenai parish.

Jean Holcomb in Homer and Pat Rowe in Seward took the responsibility in those parishes.
These women proved to be good choice in all parishes. Parents in Homer were pleased with the family program, but they wanted their children to associate with their peers. It was decided to have all the kids come one Sunday a month from two to four o'clock. Father Dean and some of the parents reviewed the

family theme, showed filmstrips or movies had provided play time and snacks

One week end a month the sisters went to Homer but stopped in Ninilchik, about forty miles from Homer for the nine o'clock Mass. The Mass in Homer was at eleven. On Monday nights they were back in Ninilchik to meet with the parents who taught their children. There were about fourteen families involved. None of the religious ed. publishers had exactly what was needed so the Sisters wrote their own programs. The big mistake the sisters made was that they thought they could use the same program in every parish. They quickly learned that each parish had its own personality and needs.

With the help of the priests and people a suitable program was made for each place. Seward is just over one hundred miles from Kenai. The sisters arrived on Saturday and attended the nine o'clock Mass on Sunday. They then drove about an hour from Seward to Cooper Landing for the twelve thirty Mass, and back to Seward to prepare for classes. Monday nights the Seward families met; and on Tuesday morning those in Moose Pass. Then it was back to Seward and on to Cooper Landing for an evening class and finally back home to Kenai.

The first year was a learning experience for all involved. Besides the basic responsibilities of supervising the religious education programs for children and training catechists, other needs evolved. Adult programs were started in Kenai and Soldotna.

People were interested in Scripture so the first classes were on the Gospel of Mark. This class was taught by the Sisters twice on Wednesdays; in the morning in Sterling (23 miles from Soldotna) and in Soldotna itself in the evening. In Kenai the classes were nine thirty in the morning and seven thirty in the evening on Tuesdays.

Both Sisters were installed as Eucharistic Ministers in all the parishes. They ministered in this way each time they were in the parish. They also brought communion to the shut-ins and the hospital patients.

In May the first year, Sister Jean Roche and Phyllis Herbert from the Mercies visited the sisters. They were given the grand tour of the Peninsula, part of which was fishing for hooligan (a small smelt like fish). Fishing is one of the things Joyce and Joan learned from the first. The Kenai River is called the "Utopia of Rivers" for good reason. It has all type of salmon, trout and hooligan. One of the things people asked them when they arrived was "Do you like to fish?" It would have been a disaster if they had said no. Fishing was and is a way of life for many Alaskans. Saying yes seemed to put people at ease and perhaps gave the impression that they would fit in.

Fish was an important food source before the road system, commercial airlines, and the increase in population. Now fishing is also a main sport and a reward. After giving retreat to high school students in Homer, Father Strass told Sister Joyce that he arranged for two teenage boys to take her fishing for king salmon, the biggest of the salmon family. On Father's small outboard motorboat they motored out of Ninilchik on Cook Inlet. A few minutes after tossing her line in Sister yelled "I got one". They boys looked at each other with raised brows. The line was in only a few minutes so they were experienced, she was not. "Sister's got a fish, ha ha!" Much to their surprise she set the hook and the fish surfaced. Wow! They became very helpful with advice and got the net ready. In a few minutes the fish was in the net. A 39 lb. king salmon! Pictures were taken, bragging was done. Sister thought, "That was easy, I can do this again". She did not do this again, many times she fished for kings over a 30 year period. It was the only king she ever caught. The main sport takes a lot of work.

Sister Joan and I feel living and working in Alaska truly put them in touch with God's wonderful gifts of nature. The first years when we stayed in the Kenai-Soldotna are we volunteered at the Kenai National Wildlife refuge. Our intention was to help in the field projects of the refuge itself. However, the staff had other ideas when they learned that we knew and liked most of the trails and had traveled all around the refuge, by foot and canoe. We were asked to work in the visitors' center to show films, answer questions and give people directions in how to get to the various lakes and picnic areas. It worked out well because we met people from all over not only Alaska and the U.S.A. but from many places in the world. We worked there until we became parish leaders; after this our free time was limited.

One of the Redemptorist Fathers who was instrumental in getting the Sisters to the Kenai was Father Richard Strass. He was the Homer Pastor. Before they came to Alaska both he and Father Wells were missionaries in Thailand. Because of this experience, when Cambodian refugees were in need of help Father Strass, through Catholic Relief Services, was asked to lead a group of parishioners to work in Cambodia. They went on that mission for six months. Knowledge of the language gave Father an advantage as well as his talent for building and organizing. Upon his return to Alaska, he was asked to be pastor in Unalaska/Dutch Harbor, out on the Aleutian chain. Unfortunately for the people out there, but fortunately for the Kenai, he was appointed pastor in Soldotna.

The first ten years of the Sisters journey were rewarding and a time of learning. The Religious Education programs in every parish were going very well and were all taught by dedicated catechists. All began to get new insights into what church means and includes. It was Vatican II in action. Many of the parishioners who arrived in Alaska after World War II were homesteaders and in some cases came before the time of established parishes. Seward was the first parish on the Peninsula and the priest there traveled to the other places when he could, which was rarely. But he always arrived at Christmas and Easter time. In many ways the people were very prepared for what happened in 1988.

Early in that year, Archbishop Francis Hurley had town meetings with the peninsula parishes to tell them we were losing one of the Redemptorist priests and there would be no replacement. He was asking for their input regarding parish leadership and to get their reactions and ideas. He was wise to consult the people and to tell them what was happening and why. People were forthright and honest in their responses and it was a profitable meeting. The day after the meeting, Sister Joyce was driving the bishop to the air port when he asked her to be administrator and Sister Joan the associate. After a moment or two of shock, not having a clue about what they would be getting into Sister agreed. Little did she realize what a new world and church was in store for them. Many thought Kenai would be the parish chosen to be without the priest because it had a commercial airport, which would be convenient for a priest coming from Anchorage. The first year a priest came every week; from the second year on it was two or three times a month. Eucharist was available because enough hosts were consecrated the week the priest was there. Kenai had the sacraments available for anointing the sick or confessions because there was a priest in Soldotna which was only thirteen miles away. Parishes in remote areas were not so fortunate. The pastors in Soldotna were all willing to go to the other places, i.e. Homer or Ninilchik for the Sacrament of the Sick. Seward had a resident priest so the Sacraments were always available. The priests in Soldotna (all who were ever stationed there) were willing to come to Kenai for Mass once a month and Sister Joyce would go to Soldotna for the Liturgy of the Word with communion. We were fortunate to have understanding and willing priests. Because of this and the openness of the people and their insights to what church really is; the Church is alive and well on the Kenai Peninsula.

Study questions:

- Do you have a reaction or opinion about how the people of the Kenai parish responded to not having a resident priest?
- What would your reaction be and how do you feel you and the parish would handle such a change?
- Would you be willing to be truly involved and responsive to the needs of the church? How?

The People of God

"But you are a chosen race, a royal priesthood, God's own people,
In order that you may proclaim the mighty acts of him who called you out of darkness into his marvelous light."
1 Peter 2:9-10

The journey of faith that took all of us in the Kenai Parish from speaking of church in traditional ways to the realization that we are church as taught by Vatican II was not easy or short.

Vatican II Constitution on the Church
"The Church, or in other words, the Kingdom of Christ in mystery…."
…the Church is seen to be a "people made one with the unity of the Father, the Son and the Holy Spirit…"
"He continually distributes His body, that is, the Church, gifts of Ministries In which, by His own power we serve each other."
After reading the Document Gaudium Et Spes many things struck Sister Joyce with regard to the laity and how they live out the Gospel in their daily lives. One sentence really stood out, (and I quote) "Since they have an active role to play in the whole life of the Church, laymen are not only bound to penetrate the world with a Christian spirit. They are also called to be

witnesses to Christ in all things in the midst of human society." Gaudium et Spes 43.

The laity are being witnesses in many quiet ways. The parish of OLA had a very vibrant RCIA program. Sister interviewed each candidate, to get to know them and answer any questions they might have. Each one was asked why they were interested in the church and how they came to the program. Without exception the answers were because of the example of one of our Catholics high principles, moral standards, kindness, and justice. The first time she heard this was from one of the men who worked on one of the oil platforms with two of the men from our parish. He told her that their high standards and how they treated others and did their jobs he felt was because of their affiliation with the Church. That was the first but not the only time she heard that. Many times they came because of the example of spouses, relatives, friends or fellow workers. This was true of both men and women. There were a few who were influenced by their reading, but they too observed the faith and good example of a Catholic lay person they associated with at work, play or within the family.

Now here are some comments from the questionnaire:

"Being church was a very foreign term in the early years of Vatican II.. However, being involved in various ministries drew us closer to our faith family and the "We are church" concept...I most always felt part of the church, but maybe not Church itself. As I became more involved, more educated in my faith I began to realize how important it was that I was and AM church.1

"I guess in the last twenty years, my definition of church has changed. Church is no longer just a building with often a visiting leader, but it is the group of people who are church; it is me that is church. Being part of this church has strengthened my relationship with God, my family and how I perceive my part in the world".2

"Twenty years ago, I thought being part of church meant the formal part of church - the Eucharist, attending Mass, following all the rules of Lent and Sunday Mass. Now I feel church is belonging to a group of people who are bonded by faith but strengthened by our kindness to each other."3

The idea of church as "People of God" taught by Vatican II was a critical part of the understanding noted by parishioners and often cited by the respondents to the questionnaire. This parishioner was especially clear: "We actually became a truly Christian Community Parish. We grew as a parish that prayed and supported our community. We not only HEARD the Gospel, but acted on it. We were empowered to BECOME the Church.4

Active participation in the parish increased. As one person wrote; "These past twenty years (with no resident priest) changed my life quite a bit. I feel like I was more in tune with my Christianity, became more giving and more aware of people's needs in our community and outside our community. Someone who was ill, someone expecting a child, someone who would be receiving a sacrament and even people in jail who were making a renewal, etc., all became part of our Christian family that we mourned with, celebrated with and prayed with."4

Another comment of note: "I don't know that my definition of church has changed, but it has brought home the reality that we are community-that church is truly the people. I have become more aware that some people cannot accept change, that there is more than black and white (grays exist), that Jesus would not get hung up on Canon Law the way some do, that the Spirit is there if we are open, that the Hierarchy needs to move to the trenches for their sabbaticals and "growth" takes a long time."5

Several people wrote that they had been struggling with the direction they saw taken by our Church leadership or with "official" Church teachings. Yet the experience of a parish where laity could take ownership brought them hope. "The breeze from the window opened by Vatican II ruffled our hair. As my own secular efforts against discrimination grew, I was recharged rather than drained by my religious practices."6

More reflections emphasize the experience of parishioners and the changing understanding of "church". Each person's reflection revealed their particular experience of the same church, the same time of change. Some parishioners came to a new understanding of "church" and their own role or part in it. They heard from their leadership a repetition of Vatican II's teaching of the "People of God", but the experience "thrust upon them" of functioning as Church without a resident priest, brought the meaning of this teaching to realty.

"In the past twenty years, I have constantly felt growth in faith and community. I am truly thankful that we were able to be a parish without a (resident) priest. We experienced great stewardship and really became church, where in the past we had been participants at the Eucharist and did what we were asked to do."7

"Everyone in Kenai was so warm and welcoming…we really felt a connection to the other parishioners and started getting more involved in things like Bible study groups, Generations of Faith and helping with Clothes Quarters and counting money. We feel like we not only belonged to this parish, but are part of the parish. We are a community. We are the church."8

Notes:
1. Linda Groleske
2. Lee Halstead
3. Therese Colton
4. Phyllis Halstead
5. Margaret Simon
6. Barbara Christian
7. Jeanette Neel
8. Karla Smith

Study questions:

- As you read the quotes from Vatican II, what were your thoughts or reactions? Did you get any new insights? What were they?
- Did any of the quotes from the parishioners resonate with you? Explain.
- How do you think you will react if or when your parish would be without a resident priest?
- Would you still believe or feel that you are still (a) church?

Ownership: What Does it Mean?

"Everyone who hears these words of mine and acts on
them will be
Like a wise man who built his house on rock.
The rain fell, the floods came and the winds blew and
beat on that house, but it did not fall, because it had
been founded on rock."

Matt. 8:24-26

In 1988 when the sisters became leaders of the
parish, they realized they needed to know more of the
parish history. One of the first things they did was read
all the minutes of the parish council saved through the
years. It was very enlightening. They discovered that
there were many decisions made that were not
implemented. The next meeting which was in the
spring, they brought them up for reconsideration. One
had to do with the renovation of the sanctuary.
Parishioners were not happy with the altar itself, it was
made of cement and looked like a huge chopping block.
Because of its size there was no room in front for the
wedding parties, the bride and groom had to sit in the
pews. At funerals we could not put the casket in front
of the altar and because it was at floor level. The altar
could not be seen if you sat in or near the back of the
church. The new administrator after consulting and
finding people would still like to renovate encouraged
them to go ahead.

The very next Sunday several of the men appeared with sledge hammers in hand and got to work. One of the parishioners designed a new altar and sanctuary furniture, another, with a talent for woodworking built the altar. We also raised it up two steps so people could see as well as hear the Mass. It changed the whole atmosphere as well as created much needed space for the weddings and funeral. It was a project begun, planned and accomplished by the parishioners themselves. This was only the beginning of the people (church) taking ownership.

In the early 90's on a Christmas Eve a group came to clean and decorate the church for the holy day. It was snowing and blowing very hard. Because the front doors opened immediately to the outside we had problems keeping the snow off. One of the men, shoveled the front steps; after the fifth time in a few hours he said, "If we had an arctic entry the steps would be covered and we wouldn't have to shovel so often and it would be safer." Covering the steps was a good idea, not only would we have shelter from the weather and cold we would have an extra room for gathering; it would also be costly. Expensive or not it was presented to the Council and proposed to the parish at large. Not only was the idea of the entry accepted, but it was decided we needed an elevator for the handicapped and it would be wise to do both at the same time. That spring the work began. We needed to raise some money; the idea of a Mardi Gras was suggested and embraced. Mardi Gras became an annual event. With people's pledges, cookie sales and Mardi Gras and a grant from the Rascob foundation the debt was paid off in three years. After, the money from Mardi Gras was used to send our youth to one of the villages to do a vacation bible school for the village children. It introduces our kids to the Native culture. Both groups learn a lot. More about this in the Stewardship chapter.

On the back wall of the sanctuary there was a large cross of cloth material that covered the speakers for the organ. It began to fray and people complained about the way it looked. It was decided that we needed something to improve the area, but what? The decision was a long time in coming. One day the door bell rang and a long time parishioner and WWII B 17 pilot came in. He sat down at the table and said to Sister Joyce, "If you don't get something done in the front of the church and I die, I don't want to be buried from here". What a shock! Sister couldn't believe her ears. Then he threw a picture on the table and said "I propose something like this." It was a picture of a church sanctuary with a statue of the Risen Christ. Then he threw a check on the table and said "This can be the first payment." After gasping for breath Sister said, I just saw a picture of the Resurrected Christ in Modern Liturgy Magazine." She got the magazine and showed him a picture of a sculpture by Suzanne Young. He liked it. The next step was to bring it to the council and liturgy committee. The decision was made; now we had to get in touch with Suzanne Young who lived in Michigan. She sent a portfolio with various statues and asked that we send pictures of the church so she could judge size, etc.. So one Sunday we put the pictures she sent on display and asked people to vote on the one they would prefer. Believe it or not, the choice was unanimous. The welcoming Jesus is now in the sanctuary.

The Liturgy committee does a wonderful job planning liturgies and decoration for the Church during the various liturgical seasons. It was decided that during advent we should not have the Risen Jesus statue in the church. After much discussion it was decided that a pregnant Mary would be the appropriate symbol. Our artists got to work and produced a beautiful silhouette of the Virgin Mary, gray on a white background that we hung in place of the statue. The banner with the advent candles and lovely tree branches made a beautiful display in the sanctuary area. We put the branches in water and lo and behold by Christmas they were sprouting green leaves; is this a sign of the Spirit coming forth or what? Everyone was delighted and somewhat surprised but it certainly raised our spirits. To be honest Sister was a little apprehensive about how it would be accepted. As usual it was foolish of her. On the first Sunday the comments were so positive; one of the most common comments were from the women, "That's what it's all about, waiting expectantly". It was another day Sister learned a lot. At Christmas we have the Mother holding the child for all to see. Now we wait expectantly for Mary, the mother to be to be in front of the church to help us realize what that holy season is all about.

This next incident begins when the parish first started. In 1953 the people of Kenai built the first Catholic church. It was a log cabin built by some of the men from Kenai as well as volunteers from the Wildwood army base which was located about two miles from the church in Kenai. After the present church was built in 1967-68 the cabin was sold. Eventually, it was used by the Salvation Army for various things. Sometime in the 90's the Salvation Army no longer needed it. Some of those in the parish who were involved in building the first church felt it would be good if we got it back. Two who were involved in the beginnings and still involved, Elsie Seaman and Leo Oberts were instrumental in making arrangements. The Salvation Army were willing to give it to us if we were willing to pay to have it moved. Elsie accepted and paid for the moving from Forest Drive to Spruce Street which is about a mile. We had a log cabin restorer come to recommend what we needed to do to restore it. He was amazed at the good condition it was in. We did need to replace about six of the logs and stain the building, put in a basement and replace the windows. As usual the people with the talents and know how came forward. We were fortunate to have Darryl (Frenchy) Payment a CCC worker from the 30's among us. He had restored and built many log cabins and knew exactly what and how we could do what was needed. He was generous with his time and expertise. The guys who helped said without him they didn't know how we could have done it. Many pitched in to help to mention them all would be impossible. However, Jerry May, Leon Quesnel, deserve credit for the everyday chores that went with the restoration. Again, though it was a parish project and many people showed up when they had anytime and could help.

We now have a tie with the past and a place for meeting, faith formation, RCIA, you name it. Again, thanks to the parish for taking ownership.

We also have an extensive outreach program. Our thrift shop, Clothes Quarters was begun in Soldotna in 1984.   After Soldotna built their new church it was necessary to move C.Q. to Kenai.   We needed to build. Again the men of the both parishes stepped forward and built a new building. To this day C.Q. provides help to all those in need not only of clothing but food, rent, medicine, you name it. It's amazing what can happen when everyone is willing to help. We would be remiss if we did not mention the fact that all the everyday things, like cleaning, laundering church linens, gardening, snow plowing bookkeeping, you name it, are all done by the parishioners.

Study questions:

- Did the phrase "taking ownership" sound new to you?
- If you consider that the parish is yours, and it is your money that is used to keep it up, shouldn't you have some say?
- Would you be willing to do as John Walsh did – face the leader and ask for change?
- When questions arise, do you come forward to give your input? Why or why not?
- How do you feel about ownership?

They Know - personal experiences of Sister Joyce

"Very truly, I tell you, unless you eat the flesh of the Son of Man and drink His blood, you have no life in you. Those who eat my flesh and drink my blood have eternal life and I will raise them up on the last day, for my flesh is true food and my blood is true drink."
John 6:53-55

A parish losing a priest has many concerns, as does the clergy and hierarchy, both very different. One concern of the clergy and bishops seemed to be, will the people know the difference between Mass and the Liturgy of the Word with Communion? They know.

The people's concern is about Eucharist and the Sacraments and when they will be able to receive them. We, the church, (priests and laity, especially parents) have taught Eucharist well. People truly believe in and hunger for Eucharist. The people in Alaska who experienced what it meant to be deprived of Eucharist and the sacraments truly hungered for Jesus and were grateful to be able to receive.

The priests who came to celebrate Eucharist also were available for the others sacraments the weeks they came. Kenai had the advantage of having a resident priest in Soldotna which is only thirteen miles from Kenai. He was on call for the sacrament of the sick and for hospital calls. The hospital was in Soldotna, which made it very convenient. Every priest was willing

and ready if we called on him. Each parish had the
Eucharist reserved in the tabernacle; therefore we could
have the Liturgy of the Word with Eucharist on
weekends or more if we wished.

  The first Communion service I had in Ninilchik in
the mid seventies really brought this home to me. Both
the pastor and I worried about how it would be
received. I learned quickly. After the service coffee was
served and we had a chance to chat. One of the
homesteaders who was with his wife told me this.
"When we came there was no parish, no priest, no
church. The priest from Seward tried to come when he
could (there was no road to speak of and they had to
boat across Kenai Lake--no small feat). The priest
always made it Easter and Christmas time. All the
Catholics gathered on Sunday nights to say the rosary.
It would have been much better if we could have had
Communion and the readings. Perhaps it takes
deprivation to help us truly appreciate what we have.
We never worried again about people's reaction; the
service was always appreciated. When we believe
nothing is more appreciated than Eucharist.

  The church teaches that Jesus is present in the
Word, the Sacrament and the community. Calling the
service "Liturgy of the Word with Communion"
emphasizes that teaching. Proclaiming the readings on
Sunday or daily keeps us focused on the seasons of the
church and the value of living the Gospel message. The
service today has a different title, but the Word, the
Sacrament and the community are still the primary

focus. Today we call it, Sunday Celebration in the absence of the Priest. This emphasizes the priest absence (as if we needed it), but the Word and Eucharist are still the most important focus.

Above it is noted that the Eucharist is appreciated and important to the community. One way this has been proven is how readily the community accepted lay presiders. All were invited by me because of their involvement in the parish and all worked at developing their spiritual lives. Our presiders were not only accepted, but truly appreciated. Their reflections were always meaningful and gave people something to think about during the week; this is what I was told every time we had a lay presider. Our presiders were three women and one man. All were trained in the rubrics and all were versed in Scripture. We had Scripture classes all through the years and all attended many of them. We also had many resources available for their use. The faith of the community and their belief in Eucharist caused them to be open to the services and praying with the community.

Let me tell you this incident to emphasize what is meant. I got a call from the hospital that one of our seniors was a patient and wanted to see me. When I arrived I was greeted with these words. "They asked if I wanted to see a priest. I said no I want to see our parish administrator." This caused me to chuckle. She went on, "You know when we were told we wouldn't have Mass every Sunday, I decided I wouldn't go when there was no priest. (She was in her eighties and said it was hard for her to get out). She was right she didn't have to go. She continued, "I did that for a couple of times and realized how important it was for me to pray with this community." She was there every Sunday. I learned a lot that day. They know.

Kenai has many visitors in the summer, salmon fishing is very important and exciting and the Kenai is called "The Utopia of Rivers". People come from all over the world; because of this we met many who never experienced the Liturgy of the Word with Communion. Many commented about the experience; all positive. One Sunday a man from Boston approached me with these words, "I know that's not Mass, what do you call it?" They know. A woman from Austria said almost the same; they know. Receiving Eucharist is important to us. The Communion Service is a big improvement over gathering to say the rosary or dashing in to receive and leaving immediately after. I used to see this when I was young and went to daily Mass during Lent, people on their way to work came in for communion, but did not stay for Mass.

People appreciate Eucharist; those moments we spend with Jesus after receiving are sacred and meaningful for us. If the official church truly believes what we have taught about Eucharist these last two thousand years how can we allow the church community be deprived of It? The Liturgy of the Word with Communion is not Mass, but the consecrated host is Jesus and we need those precious moments of God with us.

I'd like to quote a few comments people wrote of their insights of this Sacrament.

"Eucharist has always been of the utmost importance to us, but more so in recent years. If we grow in faith, we should grow in our need of Eucharist. I say need because that is how I feel. I am pretty much lost without it."

"Eucharist is what makes our Church what it is. If I could not receive Jesus in the Blessed Sacrament and in turn take Him and give Him away to everyone I meet, then there would not be much sense to my life. As long as we can have the Eucharist, we will always be church."

"Eucharist has always been important to me no matter who I received it from priest or Eucharistic Minister. That is one of the most important parts of being a Catholic."

"Life is a journey and time allows us to grow spiritually. I didn't understand as much about the Eucharist twenty years ago. It is an affirmation that we gather to worship together. We can be family, friends or strangers. Together, we seek the gifts of love, wisdom and compassion so that we might see Jesus in all people. Whatever our station in life, we are invited to come and share in a great feast. In accepting the invitation, we are enriched and renewed. We have God with us and within us. Energized, we go to love and serve God.

"My understanding of Eucharist was the bread and wine transformed into the body and blood of Jesus. Now my experience has brought me a deeper sense of this holy mystery. I see it as Christ present in our daily lives and it is in our gathering that He becomes "flesh and blood."

If I did not mention children and their insights I would be remiss, so I'll tell you my three favorite incidents if learning from children. This happened early in my teaching career, but its very pertinent today. After Mass one first Friday one of my sixth graders came in very upset. Her little brother in kindergarten (the youngest of five) went to communion. He had not made first communion (you had to be seven). Not wanting to upset the girl more I went to the kindergarten teacher and told her. Sane and sensible woman that she was, she called the child up, took him in her lap and said, "I heard you went to communion this morning." "I did", he said. "Why did you do that", she said kindly. With big eyes and huge smile he answered, "I wanted to see how Jesus felt inside." "How was that?" "Good" he answered. Is that faith or what?

Another time I was going to the altar to receive and my four year old niece was walking beside me. I felt her tug my arm. When I glanced at her she said, "He said; Take this all of you, does that include me or not?" What would you say?

Last, but not least as I was giving communion one Sunday, a girl of about ten came forward. Hearing the words, "the Body of Christ" she looked at me with a big smile and said loudly, "I know it." We know it--we believe it--we need it. What more can we say?

Study questions:

- What would you say is the difference between Mass and the Liturgy of the Word with Communion?
- Is there a link between Eucharist and praying with your parish family?
- Has your understanding and appreciation for Eucharist grown over the years? How has this affected your spirituality?
- Do you feel a need for Eucharist? Why or why not? Have you ever given thought to how your life would be if you could not receive Communion?
- There is a prayer called "A Spiritual Communion:"

Oh, Jesus, I believe in you, I hope in you, I love you, I desire you. Come, take possession of my heart.

- What do you think about this prayer? While it does not replace the sacrament, it can help bring peace. Discuss with your group.

Our Lady of the Angels Church before Arctic entry.

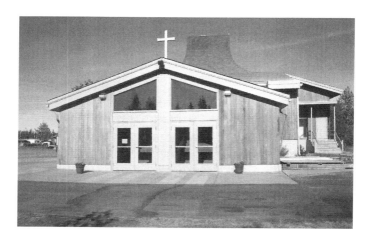

Our Lady of the Angels Church after Arctic entry
addition.

New sign with view of Arctic entry.

Sanctuary after the renovation.

Advent décor with the pregnant Mary.

Christmas with Mary and Jesus.

Christmas pageant.

Church in Winter.

Moose in our yard.

Baby moose in our yard.

Caribou behind the airport.

Moving old Church to present property.

Bear waiting for salmon at Katmai National Park.

Bear after catching salmon at Katmai National Park.

Waterwheel on Tanana River.

A gift from our mission.

The Risen and Welcoming Jesus.

Stewardship – personal experiences of Sister Joyce

"The one who sows sparingly will also reap sparingly, and the one who sows bountifully will also reap bountifully. Each of you must give as you have made up your mind, not reluctantly or under compulsion, for God loves a cheerful giver. And God is able to provide you with every blessing in abundance, so that by always having enough of everything, you may share abundantly win every good work."   2Cor. 9: 6-9

    One of the most rewarding things for me was the parish response to Stewardship. My introduction to stewardship came from my father's advice to look into it. After my mother's death, Dad volunteered in his parish of St. Madeline Sophie in Guilderland, N.Y. He was helping count the collection on Mondays. On one of my visits he said to me, "Sis, I think you ought to look into Stewardship for your parish, it's made a big difference in ours." I listened, but didn't really "hear" what he was saying until I went to daily Mass with him. Attendance had always been sparse, but this time I noticed a huge difference, instead of the priest giving communion alone, they needed six Eucharistic Ministers. I couldn't believe it. After Mass I said to Fr. Frank, "What's happened, are you getting all these people every day." His answer was "Yes, and I attribute it to Stewardship. There's been a big change since we started it." This really struck me and I took Dad's advice and planned to present it to the parish and learn more about it myself. Since our archdiocese had not started it yet, and treasure seemed to be considered the most important aspect, we decided not to push treasure but to concentrate on time and talent. This proved to be a good decision.

Encouraging people to recognize their gifts and to realize we are all gifted in some way was wonderful in that for many it opened new doors. Some did not recognize their gifts; perhaps it is just that they didn't think in terms of gifts or talents when they do something for others. Stewardship helps us to realize that everything is gift; even things we take for granted like being a good spouse or parent, preparing a good meal, smiling at someone in line at the store, you name it, it is gift. In other words stewardship gives us new insight and awareness of God, ourselves and the world around us. Using time and talent for church is one thing, but using our gifts for family and the greater community is another, it's so much more than duty.

Stewardship was embraced by the majority, many men, women and children came to an awareness of abilities they never imagined they had. Parishioners came forward to participate in and help in all aspects of parish life. Those who showed an ability to help in different ministries were invited. Many responded with "Do you think I can do that? Why?" When they were told it seemed to be their gift in spite of being surprised; they responded positively. It was and is amazing how many avenues opened and how many new things were born in the parish. Because of Stewardship we seldom had to hire outsiders to do chores or maintenance in the parish. The common response to thank you was "This is my stewardship."

Inviting people to use gifts that you recognize brings many rewards to the parish, the diocese, and the community at large. I was looking for catechists. We put it in the bulletin and asked at announcement time, but got few responses. There were two women who came to daily Mass faithfully. They had all the outward signs of faith filled persons. I decided to invite them to teach in our religious ed. Program. Both asked why I chose them to ask. I explained that it was obvious to me they had a lot of faith and I thought they could share it with our young people. That was more than thirty years ago and both are still involved in church, their gifts have been recognized by many and their involvement in the community has extended far beyond teaching the children.

We sent out a questionnaire to people who lived in the parish, but did not ask about stewardship. Yet, it was mentioned by some. Let me quote a couple of comments. The Franklins, a Coast Guard family who moved in recently, wrote, "The sisters stressed the need for everyone in the parish to pitch in and contribute to the greater good of the church, meaning the greater good of the community through enormous outpouring of stewardship. This is where we were taught that stewardship was not limited to giving money. Most of the time it was the gift of time and talent that really helped in time of need.

Susan May, who was our music director says it well: "we became Stewards of our faith. By opening so many doors, you helped us see the bigger picture. The Church isn't just a building in which we go to Mass to fulfill an obligation. Rather, it is God's people on earth sharing their time, talent and treasure. All of God's gifts to us are meant to be shared with others. The more we receive, the more we are asked to give back in His name. The more we understand the need to share, the more we want to give back. I hope that the people of OLA continue to be giving stewards."

One of the biggest blessings of Stewardship was the outreach we got involved in. The Kenai city community also benefited from the time and talent of the people. Many shared their gifts by pitching in where help was needed. Let me name a few: with youth groups (sports, scouts), Habitat for Humanity, breakfast program for the Alternative High School three mornings a week (we provided the food, cooked and served it and did the clean up), prison ministry, library, Love, Inc.. In the summer our high school youth went to a Native Village for a Religious Ed. Program for about ten days. Besides experiencing another culture, we learned the true meaning of Stewardship, our Native peoples truly know the meaning of sharing and using God's gifts wisely. We also supported a Mission in Korogocho, a huge slum area of Nairobi, Kenya in Africa. The parish has been doing that since 1983. Our parish benefited in more ways than we can count. Our church ministries were taken seriously, Eucharistic Ministers, Lectors, catechists, RCIA leaders and sponsors, ushers, greeters, sacristans, servers, baby sitters, coffee servers, you name it, it was taken care of. There were always generous, knowledgeable and willing folks to keep the property up by doing maintenance and other odd jobs. Our music directors, snow plower, lawn mowers, have donated their time, talent and treasure for years. It's been lots of time and treasure that they have given, we'll never be able to thank Susan May, Lori& J.D. Uponen, Jim Satathite and Rosemary Bird for all they have given to the parish.

In light of all this, how does the parish show accountability? First, by being aware of how people share their gifts thanking them and letting others be aware of the fact that gifts are being shared and at times telling the specifics.

With regard to the moneys contributed; we not only put into the bulletin what the collections were, but also itemized the expenses every week. People appreciated this; many expressed that they never realized the cost of hosts, missalettes and other things taken for granted in regard to liturgy. They all know about heat, lights, etc.. They are happy to know where their money goes. I must mention that we had money counters who took turns each week.

We also tried to send one or two persons who were committed to Stewardship to the National Stewardship Conference each year. At times it was a sacrifice, but it did a lot for those who went and for the parish at large.

Study questions:

- Is stewardship part of your parish life? If so, how has it helped you spiritually and how does it help the parish in general?
- When you hear about stewardship, do you think of money or gift-giving?
- How is your parish accountable to its parishioners? Do you think accountability is important? Why or why not?
- Do you think stewardship includes outreach to those outside the parish? Why or why not?

Where Else?

There are many places in Alaska without resident priests. It seems this will be true of many other places throughout the world. From experience I know this is happening in western Canada and in many places in the U.S.

We feel it's important to share some of the experiences of other leaders in the Anchorage Archdiocese, and the dioceses of Juneau and Fairbanks and Albany, NY. We'll begin with an account from Sister Marie Ann Brent, a Sister of the Holy Family from San Francisco. Cal.. Sister Marie served in both the Juneau and Anchorage dioceses.

This is her story. Sister Marie came to Alaska in 1973 and spent the first seven years in the Juneau area. She begins by saying "My belief that Church is where people gather in Christ's name to proclaim Him and to serve those in need." This was her experience as she covered the villages of Kake, Hoonah, Angoon and several logging camps.

In 1980 Sr. Marie went out to Unalaska/Dutch Harbor and once again the folks came together to celebrate, proclaim and serve others. A priest would come maybe every six or eight weeks. She moved on to Dillingham and the story was the same.

When asked about people's reactions when she arrived in Dillingham and if things changed as time went on sister Marie answered with the following story.

"I have to say, the places I've been in Alaska, the people were at least open to the idea of Liturgies of the Word with Communion and with a Sister leading the parish in the role of Parish Life Director. In Unalaska the folks had been without any Catholic Leadership or Mass since World War II. They were thrilled that someone was there and staying! In Dillingham they had a "questionable experience" the five years before I came.

I had a few who let me know they still wanted a priest, but were still welcoming.

Most were satisfied with me being there as they had no one there on and off since the 50's. The longer I stayed, the more people seemed to relish their involvement in church.

Sister Marie then moved to Valdez, a town on Prince William Sound. Sister said, "Valdez loved Father Mike and Sister Carol Ann (her predecessors). When they left, they had no leadership for about a year. The folks were wary but open when I came again, like Dillingham, the folks seem to enjoy and celebrate our present situation of leadership. That is just shy of seventeen years ago. This parish celebrates Liturgy well and when there is no priest (twice a month), unless the plane doesn't get in I share the role of presider with Deacon Dan Stowe and another lay person. We have a pastoral and finance council, a church maintenance committee, a committee from pastoral and finance who deal with stewardship, music and liturgy ministers, religious education for children, youth and adults. Our Pastoral Council has an outreach committee. I could go on and on in saying how our laity have taken owner-ship of their church and its mission, but the point is it happened and continues to happen." This is about southeast Alaska and Valdez, but we have more about the church in Alaska.

Yukon Kuskokwin Delta

        Until the year 2000 the Yukon-Kuskokwim Delta
Region was composed of seventeen bush Yupik Eskimo
Parishes in seventeen villages and one parish in the City
of Bethel. Culturally the Eskimo people are patriarchal.
After 2000 six other village parishes were added to the
Y-K Region, making for a total of twenty-four parishes.
Most were Eskimo, but one was Athabascan Indian,
which is a matriarchal culture. In the Yupik culture you
are not a complete person until you have family and
children.
        Transportation between villages is by plane,
snow machine or boat in recent times and earlier was by
dog team. Up to 2000 the Jesuits had the responsibility
for this region and only Bethel saw a priest year round.
The other parishes shared a priest with one, two three
or four villages. Since 2000, other communities of
priests and some diocesan priests have come to
minister in the region. These priests have been from
other countries, mainly Poland and Nigeria.
        Today the villages range in population from 200
to 1200, with the average village having 600-800
residence. The villages continue to share priests, seeing
them once every four to six weeks for periods of time
that range from a few days to a couple of weeks.
        In 1970 the Diocese of Fairbanks began the
Native Deacon program, which today has the name,
Rural Deacon Program. Throughout the existence of the

program men have been invited by their Parish Pastoral Councils to be leaders of prayer for their communities. From the beginning, since they were chosen by their communities, once they began doing Liturgy of the Word with Communion Services, they were well accepted as the leaders of prayer. They also perform Baptisms and witness marriages. Shortly after the Native Deacon Program began, the original seventeen parishes in the region had at least one deacon.

In order not to burn the deacons out, especially in those parishes that only had one deacon, lay people were invited by the councils to be Eucharistic Ministers who would preside at services when the deacon could not be there. Again, since they were chosen by the community and because communities were not accustomed to having a priest for "Eucharistic Liturgy all the time, these lay ministers were well accepted as leaders of prayer. Because of the deacons and lay presiders communities were able to pray together and receive Communion every Sunday and often on other days of the week, something that did not happened when only priests led services.

The communities that did not have deacons, mainly five out of six that became part of the region in 2000, selected lay people to be their leaders of prayer from the beginning; which seems to be about the early eighties. Again, these people were well accepted since they were chosen by the community and the community was now able to gather every Sunday for prayer and communion.

Some of the parishes have claimed ownership of their communities, others have the potential to claim ownership and some will slowly die out as they are mostly served by the elders with little, if any, participation by the younger generations. Currently, there are six parishes in the region that are strong, that is they function well in the absence of professional ministers and are self sustaining, except for the sacraments a priest must provide. Five parishes have some activity and leadership and have strong potential to become strong and self sustaining. Seven of the parishes have little activity and often not even services except for the two or three times a year a priest comes. We constantly hope that these may surprise us and come to life and have fuller participation by the larger community.

When we say "strong" and "claim ownership", it means the parishes have active Leadership teams composed of the local parish administrator and hopefully a local parish coordinator (these are sometimes deacons that do not hold the title but do most of the function), at least one deacon, a professional minister, and others the parish sees as important people for the leadership team. Most of the ministers are volunteers. These parishes would also have a active Parish Pastoral Council that meets even when a professional minister is not able to be present, although this is not ideal since the council is to give advice to the ministers. A catechetical program would be in place under the leadership of a local head catechist, and there would be ongoing sacramental prep done by the local people. Strong communities have a desire to be church and are willing to participate in the life of the church and larger community.

In order for the Church of western Alaska to survive, the parishes must be self sustaining. They also cannot rely on outside ministers as these come and go. The local people must own their parish and provide the ministers with will help grow the faith communities. This provides a challenge for the sacramental ministries that only priest can do since as stated above, culturally a Yupik is not a complete person unless they have a family and children.

Talkeetna, Alaska – introduction by Sister Joyce

Talkeetna is a small town on the highway to Denali National Park. It is the place of preparation for those hoping to climb Mount McKinley, the nation's highest peak. St. Bernard's Parish is there with missions in Trapper Creek and St. Christopher's in Willow.

Since the 80's these parishes have not had a resident priest pastor. Today they are served by the Parish Life Director, Renamary Rauchenstein from Talkeetna.

Talkeetna, Trapper Creek and Willow were the first places where I presided at the Liturgy of the Word with Communion. That was on January 6, 1973 - the Feast of the Epiphany that fell on a Sunday. Archbishop Joseph Ryan (the first Archbishop of Anchorage) called and said there could be no priest there and he wanted the people to be able too gather and pray on the feast, so would Sister Kathleen O'Hara and I go? This was a shock and a challenge that we were delighted to accept. Going north on January was a wonderful opportunity for us who had arrived in Alaska in August of '72. The drive up was fascinating and exciting. The snow on the mountains was spectacular and the view of Mt. McKinley from Talkeetna takes ones breath away. You truly appreciate God's creation and stand in awe-a blessing for sure.

We arrived at the trailer which was the rectory; called the designated parishioners to announce our arrival, the checked out the church. We were impressed and surprised; two city girls had a chance to check out "bush" Alaska.

We were told that a high school girl would be there in the morning to baby sit at all the places. You can imagine my surprise when I opened the door in the morning, in the dar5k, to see these two big eye brows and lashes covered with frost looking at me above a scarf and below a knit hat. It was about thirty below zero. She came in, thawed out and accompanied us on our mission. It was wonderful to get to know her and hear about living in Talkeetna. People had no problem accepting us doing the service (it was their first time, too). Alaskans are open to all new experiences and are grateful to receive Eucharist, to pray together and to be together.

It was in the 80's after their last priest pastor retired that Sister Louise Tibbets, a Holy Name Sister was appointed administrator. Renamary gives us the story from here on. "Sister Louise realized long before we did that our days of having a resident priest or sis were numbered. She made it her job to teach us to do what she was doing. Every task in the church that was requested received the answer "Well that depends. Who would like to volunteer to learn how to do a bulletin or whatever. No volunteers, no bulletin; so it went, every job was matched to a volunteer. She formed viable parish councils that met individually monthly and twice yearly the three parishes met together; each parish taking its turn to be host. We had never done this before.

Renamary was received into the church at the Easter Vigil in 1988. She became very active in the parish as lector, Eucharistic Minister, faith formation teacher, cantor, you name it; she helped whenever and wherever needed. She says "My husband, Vern, and I owned and operated a small lodge near the church and were also raising and home schooling our eight children. My involvement in Church was a much needed break from routine and I loved it."

For Thanksgiving, St. Bernard's always had a Thanksgiving Mass. Renamary mentioned this to Sister Louise. Sister was not going to be there for Thanksgiving and no priest was available. Sister said that Archbishop Hurley said it was perfectly permissible for Renamary to do a Word and Communion Service on that DAY. Renamary surprised herself by saying she would do it and it went well.

Several months later Sister injured her back. The first week she was laid up they had a priest, after that no one was available. The Bishop called and suggested that the "woman who did the Thanksgiving service" should be asked to preside. The congregation was supportive because they realized there was no other choice. But all would have preferred a priest.

When Sister was back on her feet, she suggested that every couple of months Renamary should preside in her place, just to stay comfortable with the liturgy. Rena thought it a reasonable request; when a church doesn't have a resident priest, simple things like illness, bad roads, severe weather or other problems can mean the difference between a Sunday service or no service at all.

About this time, the Archbishop introduced a program called Pastoral Leadership. It was held in Anchorage one long weekend a month. He brought professors from Gonzaga U. in Spokane, WA. to teach us about Church. The course ran for two years. It was a challenging experience and one Renamary and all who took it, especially the new administrators, we very grateful for.

The time for Sister Louise came to move on to Homer, Alaska and for St. Bernard's and the others to have a new sister. For some reason two weeks before Sister left she was told no sister was available. Sister was already committed to Homer and no priest was available. Thanks to sister Louise St. Bernard's had a strong parish council and at an emergency meeting we assured her that we would continue what she started until we were sent another administrator.

That was in August 1995. There was always a parish more in need of a leader than we were and a system of circuit riding priests was in process so the parishes without resident priests would have Mass at least once or twice a month. Once each month there was a meeting of administrators at the chancery in Anchorage; by this time Renamary was appointed administrator for the Talkeetna parish and its missions. These meetings gave us a chance to share what was happening in the parishes, ask for advice and network with those experiencing the same situations. It was very helpful for all of us.

A parish run by as lay person is very different from one with a priest pastor, Everything from Liturgy, finances, faith formation, art and the environment, music, basically everything is in the priest's hands. When a parish is without a priest pastor or sister, the understanding of church in Talkeetna began to change. We realized if we didn't pull together, we wouldn't have a Sunday service or a viable church. Since Rena was the only lay preside, she traveled to all three churches on Sunday. Now there are presides in all three churches.

The towns are small, but very much alive. All three had well established councils and at their monthly meetings planned for the coming month. They decided to form committees for liturgy, faith formation, adult ed., art and environment, outreach, and finances. Each committee is in charge of ordering their own supplies and keeping their area running smoothly. The finance committee sets the budget. The administrator oversees the whole thing, but says it runs smoothly even when she's not around. It worked very well. They had a lot of help from their canonical pastor, Father LeRoy Celementich in Anchorage. Fr. Clem kept them informed through e-mail, answered their questions and gave them a lot of support and encouragement.

Renamary still asks if the congregation has any questions doe the Archbishop they say,
"Tell him we want a priest." Today they still want a priest, but the discussion always has this stipulation; he

must understand how we operate and be willing to share the responsibility and listen to the congregation. The model of church is changing. The parishes with lay leaders have involved the congregations to the point that they feel the church is theirs. They share in the responsibility to keep her running smoothly and to be representatives of the body of Christ

Other Places

So far we've spoken of the Church in Alaska. It's true that there have always been fewer priests in the Last Frontier and the need was recognized earlier than the lower forty-eight. Today the entire church is in need of the ordained clergy. However, we have noticed that the church in spite of fewer priests is the CHURCH The faith filled laity is still practicing and are very aware that they are the Church.

There may not be as many liturgies of the Word with Communion for sacramental priests are available for Mass and the sacraments; but many parishes have Parish Life Directors. We have spoken to some and find many differences but many similarities. In other words, the people are very aware that they are church and want to gather to pray and share God's "Word and to be active by sharing their gifts of time, talent and treasure.

Both lay leaders and people want to keep the Church alive, to grow in faith and to walk in Jesus footsteps by caring for their brothers and sisters in Christ.

They have risen to the challenge and because of this and through them Jesus is present in our communities.

Albany Diocese

After leaving Alaska I came back to my community and my home diocese. As stated earlier, there are going to be more places without resident priests and led by laity. There are a few in this diocese, some have Sister Directors, some Deacons and some Laity. One of the parishes we attended, St. Vincent DePaul in Albany has a lay woman leader, Betsy-Rowe-Manning. The first Sunday we attended Mass there we thought we were back in Kenai. The spirit of hospitality, the music and participation of the community emphasized the fact we are church. There was no doubt that this faith filled community was very aware that they are church. The priest presider was very much part of this community and it showed.

There may not be as many liturgies of the Word with Communion for sacramental priests are available, but there are several Parish Life Directors. We have spoken with several and find many differences but many similarities. In other words the people are very aware that they are church and want to gather to pray and share God's Word and be active by sharing their gifts of time, talent and treasure.

Betsy Rowe-Manning was very gracious and willing when we asked for an interview and have printed many of the things she told us that truly explain why the parish is so alive and welcoming.

Betsy invites parishioners to participate in the parish activities and to share their gifts.

Invite is the key word for many are hesitant to offer when general proposals are made. (We found this to be true also). Perhaps they don't recognize their gifts or feel others could do better. However, invitations are almost always answered in a positive way.

St. Vincent's Sunday liturgies are outstanding. The choir of all ages, youngsters, teens and adults accompanied by various instruments and the entire community lifts their voice in prayer and praise. Lectors are well prepared and truly proclaim the Word. Adults and young people serve. Eucharistic Ministers graciously give "The Body of Christ".

Betsy also told us that the Liturgy Committee helps prepare the liturgies. The RCIA team works well together as do the catechists. At parish meetings, time is spent sharing prayers not just saying prayers. All seem to accept her as parish leader (one little boy said it was nice to have priests, but she was the prime minister) and work with her to keep the Spirit of Jesus alive in the everyday life of the parish. Their food pantry provides for those in need. They try to be a welcoming church to the visiting clergy and all who come to worship with them. Our experience says they succeed in this.

St. Vincent's is a parish of about 700 families, all are welcome and all are cared for.

Study questions:

- Were you surprised that there are city as well as rural parishes without resident pastors and that lay leaders were able to "carry the ball," as it were?
- Can a parish be living its faith even if there is no pastor? If not, why not? If so, how?
- Do you feel that the Holy Spirit is working in our Church? If so, how do you think we are responding?

Epilogue

Vatican II, Lumen Gentium II, 10

   For their part, the faithful join in the offering of the Eucharist by virtue of

   Their royal priesthood. They likewise exercise that priesthood by receiving

   The sacraments, by prayer and thanksgiving, by witness of a holy life and by

   Self-denial and active charity.

   The parish of Our Lady of the Angels pursued that goal under the leadership of Sister Joyce Ross RSM and Sister Joan Barina MMS from 1988 to 2009. I was one of the sacramental priests celebrating Mass one weekend a month plus one daily Mass on Thursday for thirteen years. One Sister would come with me for the Mass at the State prison every Saturday. Another priest flew in from Anchorage once a month to celebrate weekend Masses. At least two Sundays a month they celebrated the Sunday service in the absence of the priest.

   Living only thirteen miles away in the bigger of the two parishes 250 families vs. their 180 families I was amazed at all the parish life they had. From Baptismal training, faith formation for children, teens and adults, RCIA, parish socials and charity work Our Lady of the Angels was a parish where people wanted to celebrate their Royal priesthood.

They had all kinds of fund raisers to support a mission in Africa, to send some teens and adults to Mexico or remote villages in Alaska to witness their love of Jesus. The Sisters and Kenai parish volunteers were the major force for Clothes Quarters for needy folks, especially fish cannery workers. When fire destroyed the building in Soldotna they rebuilt behind the church in Kenai with volunteer help.

The Sister's were able to call forth very talented singers and musicians for all liturgies. When Sister Joyce reflected on the Scriptures people listened to a committed person of faith with years of wisdom for Catholic schools and parish work.

From the parishioners there was an increased awareness of needs to be done, like church repairs, yard work, flowers and snow removal that brought together teens and adults to volunteer for their church. I had a hundred more families, but they had many more volunteers.

My priesthood was truly enriched working with the Sisters and parishioners of Our Lady of the Angels. National church statistics show many more Sisters and laity are administering parishes and are doing wonderful ministry for the church by a powerful witness to Jesus Christ.

By Father Richard Tero, Pastor of Sacred Heart Church, Seward, Alaska

Our Hope

We hope you learned more about what it means to be church from this Alaskan account. We have no doubt that the church as People of God is alive and well. Our association with those who believe in the spiritual life and who work at their relationship with God by being church has taught us much and has helped us on our journey. God is good and the Spirit is alive and being paid attention to by this church.

It is our hope that the question "Why write this book?" has been answered by the experiences and stories of the people mentioned. We also hope that any and all who may read our account will be inspired to be church. A title suggested was "Will the Real Church Please Stand Up". In many places where the leaders encourage and allow it the church (the people) are standing up by being involved and spreading the Gospel through their action and prayer.

It is also our hope that Church leaders will recognize that is time for the real church to stand and be counted. That's one of the many things that Vatican II tried to do. In many ways it succeeded, but there is a long way to go. Let's not hesitate. If you would like to know more about Vatican II go to the Mercy website www.mercywords.com.

Sisters at Church.

WHO ARE WE?

Joan Barina, M.M. S.

I began my journey in Alaska as a Medical Technologist in the Native Health Service Hospital in Anchorage, Alaska. It was an enlightening experience - introducing me to a unique system of health care that covered the native population in their small villages in rural Alaska as well as those in urban areas. I found the native people to be warm, friendly and gentle and very artistic and creative.

A whole new phase of the journey opened with

Archbishop Francis Hurley's offer that we two sisters help with the religious education of families in the parishes of the Kenai Peninsula.

Leaving the medical lab after twenty-eight years to a completely new mission took much reflection and persuasion. Yet, as a religious woman, working for the Church and for the spiritual good of others guided my decision to accept the offer.

Sister Joyce Ross, RSM

In 1972 as a principal of a parochial school I had the unhappy task of closing the school. It was a very stressful time for parents, parishioners, teachers, priests and students. I felt I could never go through something like that again. As the saying goes, "When one door closes another opens" was true for me. Our community had opened a new mission in Anchorage, Alaska four years earlier and was looking for two volunteers. It was an opportunity to do something entirely new. Instead of going to school each day; I would be going to the parish. Luckily, I was chosen to go and a whole new world emerged. A world of beauty and a new spiritual awareness that comes from dealing with people of all ages, nationalities, careers, hopes and dreams and above all people of faith.

For seven years I worked at St. Patrick's, new parish in east Anchorage. I went there to be director of religious education, but in reality I was a jack of all trades. The staff was the pastor, a few volunteers when needed and me. We did everything, spiritually, education wise, visiting, listening, even the maintenance. My first office was over a Texaco garage/gas station. I met lots of wonderful people and got to know the area very well. There were times when the bell ringing to say "I'm at the pump for gas" (it was pumped for us in those days) got annoying, but it was also fun being over a garage and getting to know the workers and customers. We had space for classes and it was convenient for people to drop in. After a couple of years the parish was established well enough so we built our own chapel and offices.

There are lots of advantages to starting a new parish.

After seven years the bishop asked me to go to the Kenai Peninsula. There were four parishes and three missions he wanted to help and he thought sisters would help with that. The Redemptorist Fathers were the pastors and one of them Fr. Dick Strass wanted sisters. The bishop said he wanted to send two of us, no other Mercies were available. However, Sister Joan Barina a Medical Mission Sister was living with the

Mercies and was ready for a change. Sister Joan had been working at the Alaska Native Hospital. I asked the bishop if we could ask her to go with me. He said, "Work it out with your communities." We did and Sister Joan and I moved to the Peninsula in 1979.

Further Reading

1. A Church in Search of Itself – Swidler, Leonard

2. Clericalism – The Death of the Priesthood – Wilson, S.J. George

3. A New Spiritual Framework for Today's World – Reclaiming Spirituality – O'Murchii, Diarmuid. The Crossroad Publishing Co., N.Y. 1999. 370 Lexington Ave., 10017

4. The Future Church – Allen, Jr., John. Doubleday, 2009

5. Catholicism at the Crossroads – How the Laity Can Save the Church, Lakeland, Paul. The Continuum International Publishing Group, Inc., 80 Maiden Lane, N.Y., 10038, 2007

6. Common Calling: the Laity and Governance of the Catholic Church, essays by Francis A. Sullivan and Michael J. Buckley, Georgetown U. Press, Washington. D.C., 2004

7. Governance, Accountability and the Future of the Catholic Church, ed. By Francis Oakley and Bruce Russett; N.Y. Continuum, 2004

8. "On Consulting the Faithful in Matters of Doctrine", Cardinal Newman, Sheed and Ward, N.Y., 1961

9. A Presence that Disturbs, a Call to Radical Discipleship, Gittens, C.S.S.P., Anthony J., Liguori/Triumph (an imprint of Liguori Publications), Liguori, Mo., 2002

10. Tomorrow's Catholic – Understanding God and Jesus in a New Millenium – Norwood, M.S.C., Twenty – Third Publications (a division of Bayard), 185 Willow St., P.O. Box 180, Mystic, Ct., 06355, 1997

Study questions

Chapter 1: Why Write This Book?

- What do you think your reaction would be if your parish would have no resident priest?
- Have you pondered what it means to be the "people of God?" What conclusions have you come to?

Chapter 2: The Journey Begins

- Do you have a reaction or opinion about how the people of the Kenai parish responded to not having a resident priest?
- What would your reaction be and how do you feel you and the parish would handle such a change?
- Would you be willing to be truly involved and respond to the needs of the church? How?

Chapter 3: The People of God

- As you read the quotes from Vatican II, what were your thoughts or reactions? Did you get any new insights? What were they?
- Did any of the quotes from the parishioners resonate with you? Explain.

- How do you think you will react if or when your parish would be without a resident priest?
- Would you still believe or feel that you are still (a) church?

Chapter 4: Ownership

- Did the phrase "taking ownership" sound new to you?
- If you consider that the parish is yours, and it is your money that is used to keep it up, shouldn't you have some say?
- Would you be willing to do as John Walsh did – face the leader and ask for change?
- When questions arise, do you come forward to give your input? Why or why not?
- How do you feel about ownership?

Chapter 5: They Know

- What would you say is the difference between Mass and the Liturgy of the Word with Communion?
- Is there a link between Eucharist and praying with your parish family?
- Has your understanding and appreciation for Eucharist grown over the years? How has this affected your spirituality?

- Do you feel a need for Eucharist? Why or why not? Have you ever given thought to how your life would be if you could not receive Communion?
- There is a prayer called "A Spiritual Communion:"

Oh, Jesus, I believe in you, I hope in you, I love you, I desire you. Come, take possession of my heart.

- What do you think about this prayer? While it does not replace the sacrament, it can help bring peace. Discuss with your group.

Chapter 6: Stewardship

- Is stewardship part of your parish life? If so, how has it helped you spiritually and how does it help the parish in general?
- When you hear about stewardship, do you think of money or gift-giving?
- How is your parish accountable to its parishioners? Do you think accountability is important? Why or why not?
- Do you think stewardship includes outreach to those outside the parish? Why or why not?

Chapter 7: Where Else?

- Were you surprised that there are city as well as rural parishes without resident pastors and that lay leaders were able to "carry the ball," as it were?
- Can a parish be living its faith even if there is no pastor? If not, why not? If so, how?
- Do you feel that the Holy Spirit is working in our Church? If so, how do you think we are responding?

Acknowledgements

Our deepest gratitude to the people of Our Lady of the Angels who made the church real for us with their daily contributions to the life of the parish.

We would especially like to thank those who, with their time, talent and treasure influenced the writing of this book and wonderfully critiqued it;

Mrs. Margaret Simon of Kenai, Alaska, parishioner, librarian, teacher, friend;

Mrs. Valerie Kwietniak, parishioner, spiritual director, friend;

Mrs. Joyce Barina, professor of Scripture at Sacred Heart Seminary, Milwaukee, Wisconsin.

Their encouragement and help were invaluable in our ministries.

Our sincere gratitude to Rev. LeRoy Clementich, C.S.C., caring pastor, guide and friend. Also to Rev. Richard Tero, canonical pastor and friend. Their input to this effort was very special to us.

Special thanks to Kenai parishioners Susan May, Leonard Efta, Gerry May, Leon Quesnel, Darryl

"Frenchy" Payment, Dan Sterchi, Jim Satathite, and George Shaw. These volunteers were instrumental in the renovation of the sanctuary and in restoring the old log church, as well as contributing ideas and muscle power to the general maintenance of the parish buildings.

So many parishioners (so little space) contributed so many ideas, gifts, so much time, so much caring. You know who you are, so do we – Thank you!

Other Parish Life Directors who work in leadership roles in the parishes and contributed to this book have our gratitude and prayers;

Sister Marie Ann Brent, Holy Family Sister and co-worker from Valdez.

Sister Kathy Radish and Sister Ellen Callaghan, Franciscan Sisters from Yukon-Kuskokwim Delta.

Renamary Rauchstein, Parish Life Director from Talkeetna.

Betsy Rowe-Manning, Parish Life Director at St. Vincent's from Albany, New York.

We would be remiss if we did not mention the encouragement and support we received from our communities, The Medical Mission Sisters and Sisters of Mercy. We truly appreciate Sister Martha Joyce RSM and Sister Maria Hornung MMS for their editing, input and encouragement. Angela Gaffney and Joan Lamar, the communication people of the Northeast Mercy community, gave excellent advice and their editing skills were most helpful. Chole VanAken who helped us with the set up and transferring the photos to CD's and ultimately to the book. Graham Macbeth was most generous giving of his time and talent in helping with the computer work. Without him we may not have had the final result. Our gratitude and prayers for all who have helped us.